I wrote this Instead of Crying

KINJAL MARU

AF518981

BlueRose ONE.com
Stories Matter
NewDelhi • London

BLUEROSE PUBLISHERS
India | U.K.

BlueRose ONE
Stories Matter
NewDelhi • London

For permissions requests or inquiries regarding this publication, please contact:

BLUEROSE PUBLISHERS
www.BlueRoseONE.com
info@bluerosepublishers.com
+91 8882 898 898
+4407342408967

ISBN: 978-93-7139-578-6

Cover Design: Aman Sharma
Typesetting: Pooja Sharma

First Edition: September 2025

Author's Note

This book is split into two parts: ***Rainbow and Reality***, because honestly, aren't we all caught somewhere between the life we wish for and the life we actually live?

I've been writing my feelings into words for years.

This book holds those feelings—messy, honest, and a little all over the place, just like life.

I've always been a bit confused soul.

I could never really decide what I wanted—whether it was about my career, my friends, or even my own heart.

But the one thing I've always been sure of? Writing. That's where I always find myself.

This is the story of someone who feels everything a little too deeply, who's soft, a little chaotic, and still figuring things out.

Maybe you'll find pieces of yourself in these pages too.

This is my first collection, created in place of tears and joy. I live between dreams and deadlines, always chasing stories that feel like home.

— Kinjal Maru

To my Parents,

Who blessed me with amazing life I owe you everything...

To my Sibling Aayushi and Sneh, Thank you for your existence

To my husband Dhruv,

Thank you for encouraging me to finish this shelved project, it would not have finished without your constant support.

To my Friends Komal, Nihar and Tanvi, thank you for being raw and unfiltered.

I love you All!!

This isn't just ink.
It's every moment I didn't break.
Every breath I took when I thought I couldn't.

RAINBOW

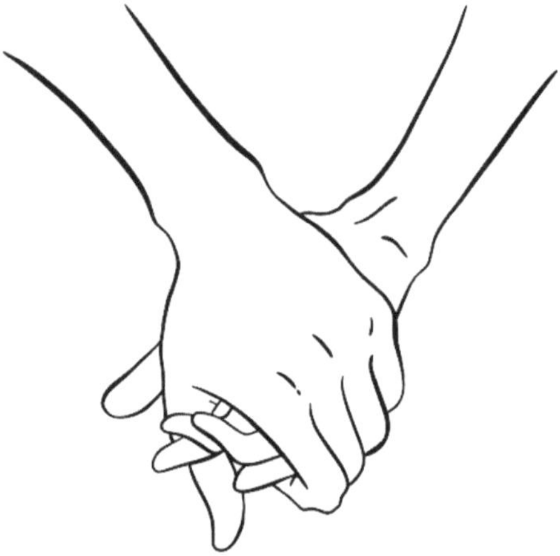

I wanted you to become my rainbow,
but you got afraid of the thunder.
I longed to drench you,
with the rainbow of my love
but you got afraid of the rain.

Dear future husband,
The journey of looking for you
Started when I was very young
Let me blame all fairytales for it
My first love, felt like forever
Until he shattered my dreams into pieces repeatedly.
Only to break my heart deep now,
I collaged my broken pieces into a rainbow again,
Only this time, it was for me
My rainbow is still bricks and walls,
but I know,
I will have all the colors in it,
all the colors, in a lifetime.

You and I are lovers,
In a parallel universe...

Life is the sun,
love is the moon,
and we,
we are somewhere in between,
chasing sunlight
with shadows in our hands.

You are my place, my home,
The place that brings out the soul in me.

Peel my skin, stitch yours on me
make me yours,
let me carry your scent,
Let me feel you
even when you're far away.
Wrap me in your silence,
hold me in your absence,
be the shadow that lingers
when the night grows cold.

If I could fold the sky in half,
I'd keep one side for you and one for me,

and in between, we'd dance on stars
and sleep on verses of moonlit poetry.

My heart is a canvas,
for you to paint your love.
Soft strokes of morning kisses,
shades of laughter in the sun.
Let every color you choose be a whisper of forever,
a masterpiece only we understand.

You brought an ocean of love
Into my emptiness,
I swam in it,
Without the fear of waves
I was floating, I felt light,
The exact love I ever needed.

They say falling hurts the body, but falling
for you healed parts of me I didn't know were broken.
They say falls leave scars,
but yours felt like a blessing,
the kind that touches soul, not skin.
They say falling bruises the body
But falling for you softened the ache in me
They say falling is bad for the body,
but falling for you was the only pain
I'd choose again.

No endings, no alarms,
just you and me,
lost in a dream
we never had to wake up from.
This,
This is life at its best....

Your love was like music to my ears
Sometimes it was soothing,
most of the time, it was loud.
You were never just a song.
You were my whole playlist of moods
I didn't know I could feel,
a rhythm that lived inside my heartbeat.
But like every playlist,
it ended.
And now,
even in silence,
I still hear you.

One day,
Someone will love you
with all the fire within
not to tame you,
but to burn with you.

And that, my friend,
will be the end of your suffering
Not because love saves you,
but because it sees you,
exactly as you are,
and chooses to stay in the heat.

With the power vested in me,
I pronounce you mine
always,
and forever.

"Christmas tree love"

love me like a Christmas tree,
let the lights shine on my body,
decorate every inch of me with your hands,
Claim me as your own,
celebrate me, that's the kind of love
I want to explore
kind of love, kind of lust...

I hope you find love again,
the kind that is gentle on your skin,
that doesn't feel like a battle
You must win...
I hope it doesn't ask you to shrink,
to break, or to bleed for it.
I hope it sees you,
All of you,
and stays anyway.
And if nothing stays,
I hope ***you*** become that love
for yourself first.

You were like my poems, DREAMY.

Every day,
I carry the weight of my rainbow,
a baggage of insecurities, a package of flaws,
With little more hope and wishes
and when I decided
to let my rainbow fly in the direction of self-love,
I suddenly felt my wings get lighter
I flew with love in my heart
and was welcomed, open-armed
The embrace was so powerful,
my eyes melted into tears
but I loved it,
That is what I needed

I love simple pleasures.....
your hands tangled in mine,
your lips tracing my skin,
and your soul soaked in my love.

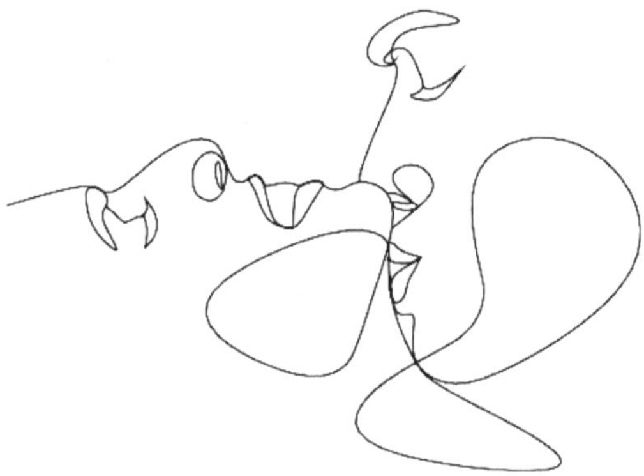

When I first fell in love,
I wanted it to be an adventure
naive, brutal, raw,
and dramatic in every way.

I chased that chaos
like it was the only kind of love worth feeling.
I romanticized the hurt,
believed pain meant depth,
and wore heartbreak like a badge.

Repeatedly,
I gave pieces of myself to the wrong stories.

But then I fell in love again
This time, with the right person.

And I realized:
you don't have to chase chaos
to feel alive.
Sometimes,
Peace is the wildest thing
you'll ever allow yourself to feel.

I want to wear your love,
like a piece of jewelry

No one really sees
the kind of strength it takes
to trust again
It's the softest kind of courage
to open your heart
with trembling hands,
and still say:
"Here. Take this.
But please, be gentle."

Darling,
I'm not a Book
I'm a library, vast and deep,
You will ***Lose*** yourself in
my pages....

Let's not pretend something doesn't bother you, let's
Not pretend that isn't hurting you, let's not pretend
that someone isn't getting under your skin,
It's okay to show your vulnerability,
It's okay to show your emotions, it's okay to show your true self,
It's fine, it really is fine,
It's normal it is YOU!

I realized,
No one in this world is ever going to love me
like my sister does.
In the quiet way she checked,
if my pillow was wet the morning after we fought.

Be in love with yourself,
be authentic,
be kind,
be whatever you want to,
but never choose to be
someone you are not proud of.

Your desire to be loved,
Should never die...

Today I Choose Sunlight

The coffee in my hand and soul searching at the end!!

"Peace over everything else"

She held my hair back,
not just in sickness,
but in heartbreak,
When grief came pouring out in sobs I couldn't name.
She didn't ask for explanations,
she read the tremble in my voice like poetry,
and knew exactly where the pain lived.
We've undressed our souls in midnight conversations,
where silence wrapped around us like a blanket,
and healing sounded like
"I'm here"
and meant it.
She is the mirror that doesn't distort,
who sees the girl, the woman, the fire,
and still loves all of it, without needing a reason.
Ours is not just friendship,
It's a soft, sacred intimacy
that needs no performance,
only truth.

They said she was "too much,"
as if power in a woman
was a flaw to be trimmed.

The peace that is brought by your favorite person
should be untamed by any storm in your life.

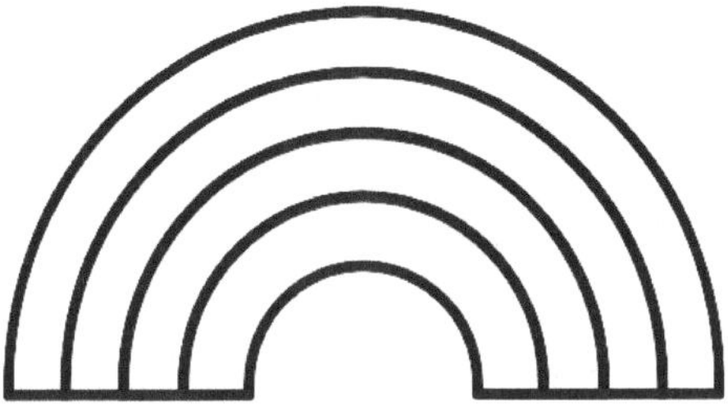

My soul is searching for the rainbow
that is brought after the storm,
only to be drawn again,
like a child tracing hope with trembling hands.

She does not ask for space,
she becomes it.
She does not chase light, she
is it.

There should be no shame
in wanting to be heard
No shame, needing to be held
It's okay to break sometimes,
Vulnerability is not a crack,
It's the doorway to something real.
To crave affection is not a flaw,
It is the heartbeat of being
only humans.

Your heart is the only ladder to climb a
Mountain of Love

Maybe our *Love* was always written
in the quiet between galaxies,
two souls orbiting.
Your hand fits mine like
we've held constellations together,
Like stars remember us.

I am the voice that said, "Enough,"

My past is not a cage,
It's a garden.
And every scar I wear is proof:
I bloomed anyway.

"*My Darkest Ally*"

No one stood harder for me
than my depression.
It showed up when no one else did,
sat beside me when the room emptied,
and held my hand.
It made a home out of my hollowness.
And though it hurt me, broke me,
kept me in prison,
There was a time when it was the only thing that never left.

I am learning
to build a new House,
not of broken bricks,
but of the pieces I've collected
through healing.
A place where love doesn't just stay,
it grows.

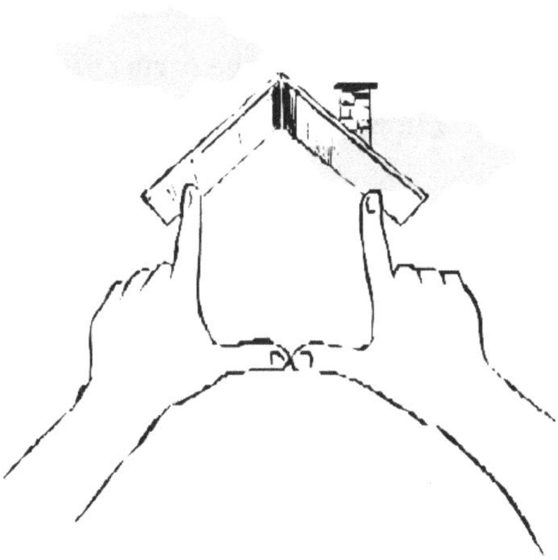

Our First Time

You touched me with trembling hands,
Like you were learning me, like this was new.
And I knew… you'd done this before.
But with me, you felt like a fresher,
and it was cute.

It felt comfortable.
I let you near the parts of me
I never dared to see myself.
Not even in mirrors.

With you,
It didn't feel broken.
It felt… holy.

You were gentler than I'd ever known.
Like softness was a language you wrote just for me.

It felt so good, not just in body, but in soul.
Like we were being knotted into one quiet moment, our bodies aligned,
our hearts slowly entangling.

Life with you feels like a movie, imaginary,
Yet somehow the most real thing
I've never lived.

I am both chaotic and calm,
a storm before the rain, and the quiet night that follows.

It depends on the mood.

I am both, and I am enough.

I hope you never saw our love as a failure,
because it never was.

We failed, not our ***love***.

In my mind, we're still together,

chasing all the dreams
we once whispered under stars, hand in hand
in a world that never broke us!!!

Some days, I want to be loud
to scream my name into the sky just to hear it echo back,
to know I still exist outside of what I do for others.
Sometimes, I lose myself
trying to bridge the gap between people stretching my heart,
It's heavy, carrying what no one sees, wearing a smile
while my soul slouches underweight.
I just want someone to hold my burden for a few seconds,
so, I can breathe,
So, I can feel light again, even if only for a moment.

One day,
This distance will be a story we tell how we stayed soft,
how we stayed sure, how even the stars knew
We were always meant to find our way back home.

You are allowed to pause, to fall apart quietly, and still be whole.
This is good

It's a gentle reminder we all need sometimes that broken doesn't mean broken forever, and softness is strength too.

Undress me not just the clothes,
but the parts I hide in daylight
Let the room witness how I turn into fire
Beneath the weight of your wants.
Speak with hands, answer with breath, and don't stop until I forget
where I end and you begin.

If our love is fiction,
may I never reach the final page...

And never, ever
be less under anyone's influence.

I love you from the past,
the version of me who still believed in us,
in magic, in something softer than silence.

I am too tired to speak,

but my thoughts scream louder in my head.

I sit in silence,

while a storm tears through me, unseen, unheard.

I wonder, how is it

that the whole world seems to have a problem with me, and I carry none for them?

Why is it always me breaking myself into smaller pieces

just to keep the peace?

What is this world of expectations, where they built towers of their needs and crushed mine without even looking down?

sometimes,

The simplest moments are the loudest miracles

I'd choose you in a crowded room,
in silence, in noise,
in every version of this life where we exist...

When you're with the right person, they don't just see you,
They awaken a version of you you've never met.
A gentler fire, a softer strength,
a laughter you didn't know lived in your chest.
They don't complete you, they reveal you

You didn't save me, you sat beside me, while I saved myself.
And somehow, that meant more
than anything else could.

We were poetry in the wrong book,
a perfect line in a story
We couldn't finish.
Still,
I read you in every silence.

I will write to you in the wind

Words that never reach but still mean something. You live in a time zone I've learned by heart, and every sunset here

is a sunrise to you.

That's how we hold hands— through sky.

I was taught to stitch my rainbow
Only remember how you tore it first!!

The world keeps saying love shouldn't be this hard.
But then again, they've never had you.
They've never waited for a voice to feel like home.
They've never stayed, even when staying meant staying apart.

God could not be around, so they created mom,
and they could not guide you, so they created female friendships
In the world to show me what love can be...

Because love like ours doesn't fade in absence, it grows,
like roots beneath the frost, waiting for spring....

Be softer with yourself,
You are a goddess no one believes....

I hope one day
we choose the same path, same ways to find each other again
I will wait at the same spot, our spot,
waiting for you to catch the same usual train,
a day when our eyes meet again, you will gaze at me from the crowds, and I will pretend I never noticed,
to find each other again, to find the forbidden love, until then,
rest in my dreams.

you are allowed to slow down.
Even the moon takes nights off from shining.
Even the sea knows when to retreat.
You, too, deserve that softness.
Not for what you do but simply
for being *YOU!!!*

You didn't deserve what broke you.

And you don't have to keep breaking yourself to prove it.

And then she said YES!!

(to becoming a poem written by her own hands)

REALITY

Once upon a time,

A rainbow of love decided to glow in my heart, the one who let me bloom around the world, the one who made me feel whole,

I felt he was the cure of my insecurities, I didn't miss my flaws,

I was whole myself,

The distance didn't touch the connection, it was so pure and raw,

conversations were touching, thoughts were naked,

Life felt real, but one day,

He decided to be honest,

honest about his attachment to me and we realized

It wasn't our time to shine!!

You loved the fire I was,
until it burnt you, inside
out.

I tried to calm my chaos, and found myself trapped in thunder

No amount of effort and love could storm into you

Then, I realized!!!

Something which is not describable,

Just like your love

"Loud but Empty"

I deserved all the hatred, all the cries, all the pain,
I wanted our love to be thunder, trapped in a glass bottle,
Where no storm could touch us
I loved you with all I had
To learn,
It was the end of everything.

I Bloomed, I bloomed in your love, I bloomed in your presence,
I bloomed as a flower, in the cold weather
I bloomed as a rainbow, in the summer.
All unrealistic, but dreamy, dreamy like my thoughts for you.
The only thing is dreams are forever
But you were not.

At the end of the day, I think we're all toxic in some way. Maybe not with bad intentions, but through silence, selfishness, or the stories we twist to make ourselves look better.

You're telling me you've never faked kindness?

Never wanted to hurt just so you'd feel less alone in your pain.

Never broke a heart and told yourself it wasn't your fault?

No one is entirely pure.

We all carry a little shadow, a little bitterness, a little guilt.

The truth is your toxic trait is just the part of you, you're not ready to admit exists.

you cannot love someone unconditionally, even love has its limit,
You are a fool if you think effort will save your relationship,
you cannot change if a person's heart isn't there, let them be free,
They were always the butterflies, finding new flowers every day.

I spent my life, building walls around my heart, wondering someone would break it, I spent my life, watering dead plants, Wondering it would bloom, I spent my life, searching for affection in dead attachments And crushed my soul in the process.

How do you expect people to be honest with you, when you are struggling with being honest with yourself??

I got an empty space in my heart, wanting to be filled by you, The depth of my emptiness is ready to drawn you into my world, The Black hole of my love is bad for your survival, But let's take a deep, lets wave, lets swim into it, Let us drive the madness of our love into sea, and wait for the hurricane.

Some people leave scars in your life, mind, body and soul, that is unforgettable, no amount of love, care, attention can cure it,

but at the end of the day when you sit down and wonder what you did to deserve this

You get no answer, that my friend is, real shit pain...

You said forever like it meant something. Like it was carved into the bones of time,

like it could survive silence, storms, and sleepless nights.

But look at me now, talking to ghosts, begging the air to remember your voice.

Was it all a performance for you? Because I didn't need rehearsals.

I bled in real time.

You held me like I was fragile, then dropped me like I was forgettable. And I'm supposed to be okay with that? I'm supposed to carry that kind of ache in my chest and still wake up, still smile,

still say "I'm fine"?

Say it wasn't all a lie.

Tell me, just once

that some part of it was real. That when you looked at me,

You saw something worth staying for.

That I wasn't just a chapter you couldn't wait to finish.

Because if I was only a pause in your story, why did you feel like the ending of mine?

When it was my time to bloom, I again let everyone walk over me.
Result: Crushed.

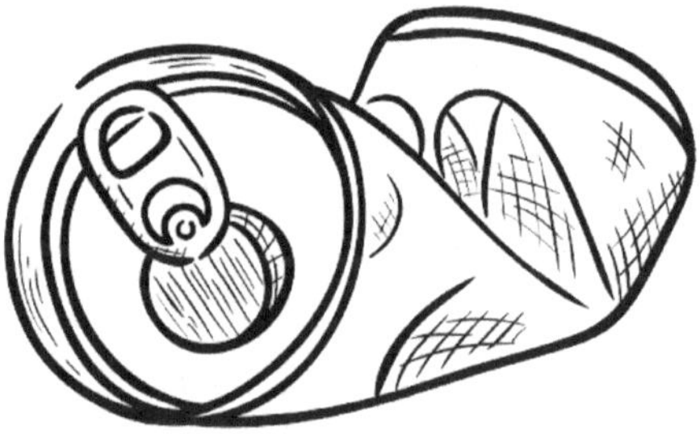

I wish people were okay showing vulnerability, it shows you care, you aren't weak,

It shows you have emotions, strong enough to be told, it shows you are brave,

It is a strength, do not let that feeling go.

I used to rewind it all, trying to understand how love could turn into betrayal,

how someone who once held me could so easily let go.

But now I see it clearly you didn't break me because I wasn't enough. You broke me because you couldn't face your own emptiness. You needed someone to carry your guilt, and I happened to be the one soft enough to do it.

But not anymore. I've stopped bleeding for the wounds you created. I no longer need closure from a person who was too cowardly to offer honesty. I'm learning to choose myself fully, fiercely, and without apology.

I have scars left on my inner peace...

I found myself finally, Finally, I bloomed, I bloomed like lava in the month of December

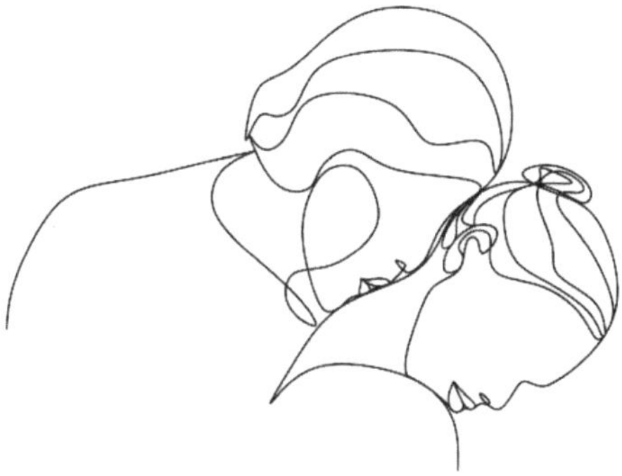

He was my everything, still my heart skipped a bit to reject the gorgeous face kneeling down in front of me, maybe he was everything, but I was not myself around him..

There is this thing in being emotionally attached, it allows you to feel the pain and pain that your heart thinks it deserves.

Don't believe in *Kindness is free* crap,
Your energy should be protected in all ways,
Never waste yourself in temporary souls.

I am a bee, stuck in my rainbow Wondering how I will be a butterfly

Don't believe in Vibes, Vibes lie, Vibes are not permanent, Vibe is a feeling, not the end,

People change, Vibe changes...

What is the purest form of love, you think you deserve?

I am a peace, and I am a storm,
It is on you, which side of me is taking a toll on you.

I am just a lost bag of burden, which no one wants to claim

I found someone more interested in my soul than my body,
I got afraid to show my real self, my fear sabotaged our love,
Once again,
I let love pass over my insecurities...

"Peeling"

It's easier to peel your clothes for love than to de-layer your soul

I am an introvert at home

I am an extrovert to the world I am traumatized in real life

I wish I had a concealer for my heart
to lighten my darker soul

I am a dustbin of emotions
for people to throw their garbage of opinions
about me.

love and sea are so similar the resemblance

can't identify when they're far but the depth of it

can scare you

one is the depth of an end, and one is the depth of feelings both are scenic in their ways

The whale of emotions has all the capacity

to kill your soul

but also has the capability to free your mind

I hoped I would find something I was missing
I thought my void would be filled hoped I would find love again
every day I gave myself to him
a little more willingly,
I gave my heart my soul
my body and now, my sanity
parts of me are dead while he bloomed
I am left with nothing, and he is blessed
With my love
I am left with scars on my body and soul
and all I was trying to cover was his negligence
towards me

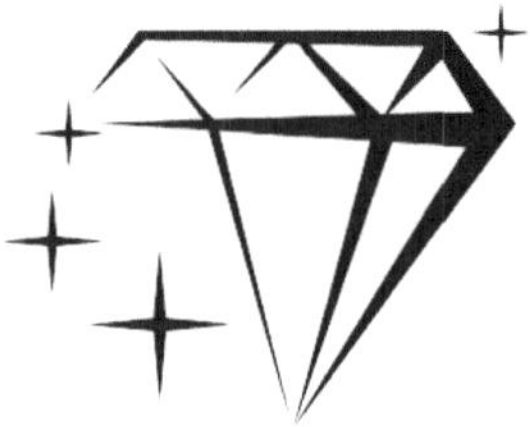

My dad made diamonds like how he made me with love,
affection, and care,
The only difference was every cut sharpened its shape and here
It wounded my soul.

It's not easy
to open with your people, it's not easy
To pour your heart
It's okay if you can't express yourself in the way you want to,
Showing your true self won't scare away the people who are meant to be in your life, they'll find a way to bond, in any circumstance and that's how you gain faith in yourself and in people.

I will mourn your absence rather than
being unfaithful to me.

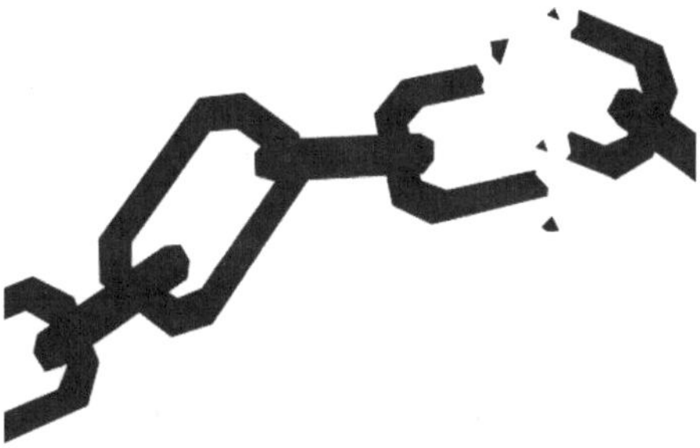

It's okay
to detach from people life isn't always
about giving second chances it's also okay
to miss them
It's going to take time but one day
You will feel fine, wait for that day, the sun will rise
in your direction and everything
will feel normal again.

Sometimes

I wish I could be

as vulnerable as I want without fearing what it will cost me,

Sometimes I wonder if I even remember what it's like, to not feel broken, what scares me most is the quiet thought that whispers, what if this is how I'll feel forever?

One thing about time is so irritating that
it passes quietly,
like it's doing you a favor, but healing doesn't follow patterns,
It's mostly about pretending, carrying what no one else can see.

There was this time in my life, where I felt stuck writing, people call it writer's block, but I don't think so!! I had thoughts but was unable to put them into words, the change has been after I was Married, they say when you are happy you can't seem to focus.

Is that true????

"focus"

Life would have been easy if I knew where to focus,

who is going to tell me?

I am in a mentally stable place right now but still

There are days the past taps on my shoulder and the trauma answers for me

I remember when I couldn't cope

when breathing felt like breaking when death didn't feel far and nothing made sense

Even now I get scared of falling back from breaking again

Why do I feel like I don't deserve happiness?

Why does my own mind try to sabotage

the things I prayed for.

Why do I feel that?

I want to be irreplaceable, Period!!

Why does our whole life purpose is to find meaning to our lives??

Instead meaning is something we create through what we love, who we become, and how we respond to pain, beauty, and change.

Different thinkers have different frames!!

They told me to go out,
And find the meaning of life so I wrote my pain,
into poems and found it in every line,
I thought no one would read.

The World Profits from our insecurities and we keep feeding them!!!

I want to be the diamond, shaped by love,
but no longer cut to fit someone else's vision of me

What is more poetic love, anger or hurt??

At the end,
It's the love we give, the hurt we carry, the dreams we chase
That might never catch us, yet we run,
With the faith that maybe, one day, they will.

What is your opinion about life but in a poetic version??

For me,

Life is both the question and the answer, the silence and the song,

the everything and the nothing, it's all at once too much,

and yet, just enough.

Life is the dance of the earth and the stars, forever in motion, yet never still.

It's the question we ask in every heartbeat, and the answer we discover every fall.

It's both the weight we carry, and the wings that lift us.

It's too loud and too soft,

and in the middle, we learn to listen.

Proving yourself is like chasing shadows,

an endless race to a finish line that keeps moving.

It's the weight of expectations,

piled high on shoulders that never asked to carry them.

We seek validation in the eyes of others,

as if our value could be measured in their gaze,

but in this chase, we forget the only gaze that truly matters is the one we give ourselves.

Why the rush, you ask?

Maybe it's the fear of being unseen, the fear of being misunderstood, a fear that we're not enough,

But the rush, it's not about proving the world wrong, it's about proving to ourselves that we are worthy,

worthy of love, worthy of respect,

worthy of being seen without the need to explain.

But in the end, the truth is simple,

You do not need to prove anything to anyone but yourself.

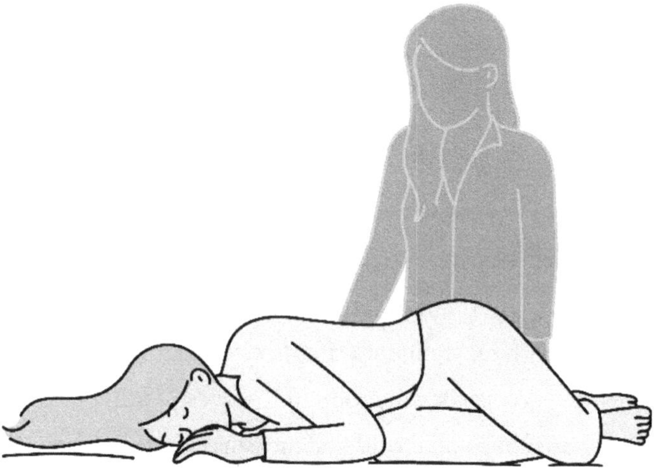

Life without love is not truly life at all, it's a journey without a destination, a flame without warmth, a soul without a home....

Love is the thread that binds our hearts, the light that guides us through dark times, the hope that makes us believe

that even in the hardest days, we are not alone.

The soul inside me feels dead, drenched in silence,
yearning for rain.
I wait for the storm, for the cleansing drops
that will bring me back to life.

My dear, you are doing the bravest thing,
by just showing up.

What is love? Is it a word, a feeling,

or someone you name as your whole world?

How can one person be the definition of love

Your home, your calm, your chaos?

How does someone become the reason your mood shifts, your work suffers,

Your heart aches?

But darling, it's not your fault.

You handed them that power because your heart is full.

Full of love. Full of hope.

You see the light in others

and pour warmth into their emptiness.

You cook for them, care for them, give your body,

your undivided attention.

And all of it, for what?

To be betrayed?

Healing is such a lengthy process,
It is like you are in your happy place,
and
All a sudden a rush of emotions from your past peels your skin deep enough that all the previous wounds are fresh again.

Some wear love like a broken shield, Wounds exposed yet never healed.

Some wear love like lipstick, bright, bold colors painted over fight.

Some choose toned shades, soft and kind, to soothe a trembling, restless mind.

But in the end, beneath the art, we all hold love in a heavy heart.

I don't have answers, only echoes,
soft ones, that sit beside me
when the world goes quiet.

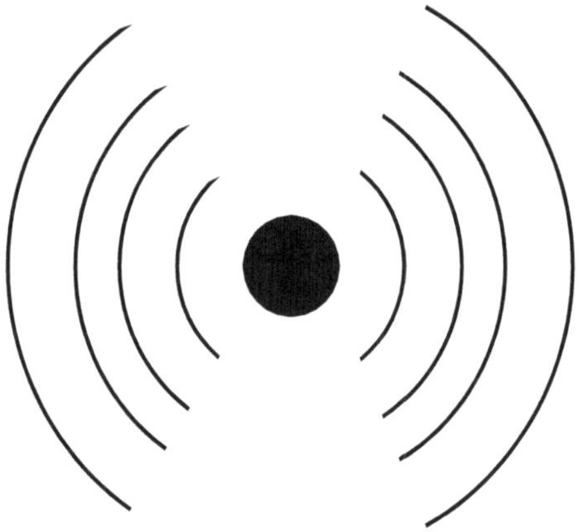

Some days, the soul is quiet.
Not broken, not whole, just still.
Not every feeling has a name, and that's okay.

In a world that always wants more, stillness is a boundary,
A place where you can say, "*I am enough just as I am.*"

Life is strange
We silence our own voices to turn up the volume
on someone else's opinion.

we hush our hearts to hear their noise, as if their words
were more worthy than our own.

Is it cruelty
if my hands stay clean but my heart stays bitter?

I have always lived between love and loathing
Some days,
I worshipped the curve of my waist, the way my hips
refused to shrink for anyone's comfort.
Other days,
I stood in the mirror wishing my skin was someone else's.
I wanted to feel pretty... whatever that meant but some mornings,
I chose peace over polish, and silence over the scream to be enough.
This body,
it holds me still, even when I'm the one
trying to leave it.

I remember Every Wound, Every Scar,

Reminder of your existence in my life I call them!!

Let it remind you
You are not behind, you are becoming.

The ones who hurt me started tripping

on their own patterns.

I didn't have to wish them harm they were already haunted by their own reflections.

I learned Karma doesn't need a witness.

It's not revenge.

It's release.

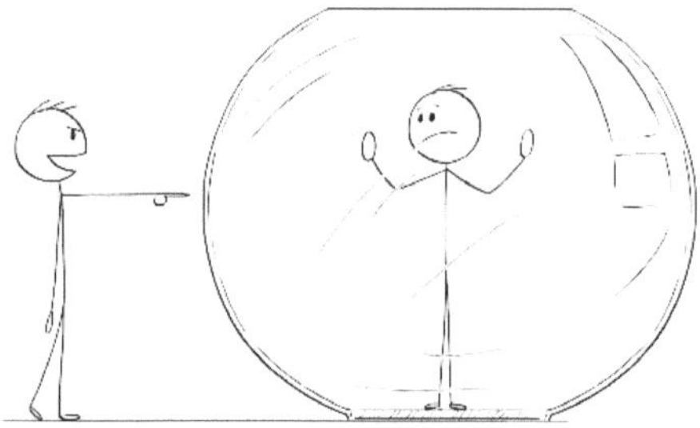

"Is It Still a Sin?"

Sometimes I wonder, are my sins forgivable?
The ones I don't speak of,
but feel burning in my chest like secondhand guilt.
Is it wrong
that I wanted to hurt the one who made me feel small,
who found the softest part of me and bruised it
just because they could?
I secretly hope life teaches them what they taught me.
They say don't wish bad on others, but what about the nights
you lay awake, not wishing, just waiting?
And if justice comes, not from my hands,
but from somewhere beyond me is that still wrong?
Or is that just how the universe restores balance?

I take rage,

and press it into pages until it burns with meaning.

Healing doesn't always arrive with calm hands,
Sometimes, it whispers through tears when
you thought you were done crying,

but healing isn't a race. It's a quiet choice,
To believe there is still light worth walking toward.

I thought love would feel like home warm, open,

where I could rest and heal.

But how do you find comfort when the walls you grew up with are built from doubt,

agony, ignorance, and self-doubt?

I didn't know any better.

So, I brought that kind of love into my life,

expecting it to fill the empty spaces, to feel familiar.

I wish there was
a thing called chasing reality because dreams,
they slip through fingers.

Still Writing to You

See,
My love for you is so strong, I'm still writing about you in agony,
while you're long gone....

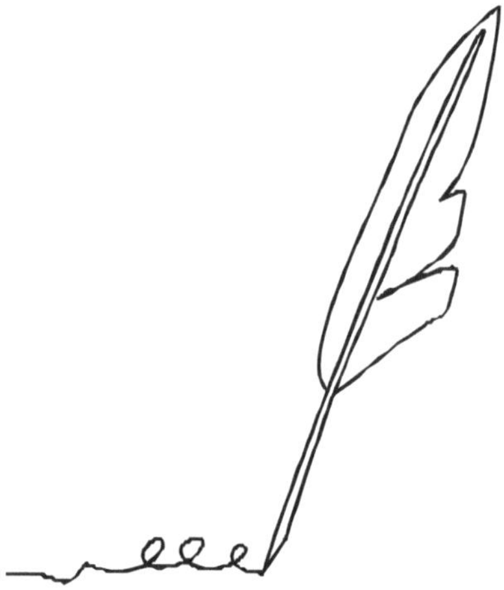

"Too Much"

I have a love-hate relationship with my food.
It's either a full plate or just a lonely morsel. There is no in-between, only guilt or hunger
and the voices that come with both.
Some days,
I crave a flat stomach, trace my fingers across curves
and wonder what it would feel like to take up less space.
My heart pleads, "Don't think, just eat."
But my mind whispers, "Stop. You've had enough."
I am too much.
Too much weight, too much skin,
too much of everything and all.
And yet, somehow, it is not enough to feel at peace in this body.

I stitched my loneliness into a velvet dress, wore it like confidence.
Everyone applauded the fit.
No one saw the seams.

They said I was radiant.
I said, "Grief" glows too.

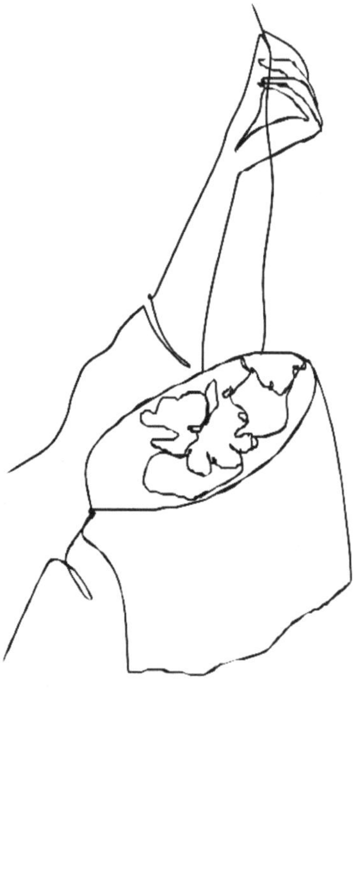

My insecurities
are stitched into my skin.
Now, it pains
To untangle them!!

It's hard to hold someone's love
when your own hands have never learned how to hold yourself.

As a child,
I faced siblings like rivals, competing for love
I thought I had to win.

Little did I know,
This battle would follow me, insecurities tangled tightly, woven deep into my heart.

I want to believe that

I was the ***Love*** of your life!!

It's funny how you say
Your love for me remains the same, but when I look behind,
All I see is how much has changed.

I wish you had left in one piece,
like a bandage ripped in a second.
But no,
you left in fragments, only to return
when my wounds had barely scabbed.
I'd press ointment to the pain, pray for silence,
but you'd come back peeling me open again, and I'd shatter,
just like before.

Why is what I think, and feel is an entirely raging sea,
while you see just a drop of water......

Dented, Not Broken

I am fragile,

but not shattered-glass fragile.

More like a favorite mug chipped at the rim,

a little stained by time, yet still warm with hope. I may not gleam like new,

but I still hold what matters.

And that, is more than enough.

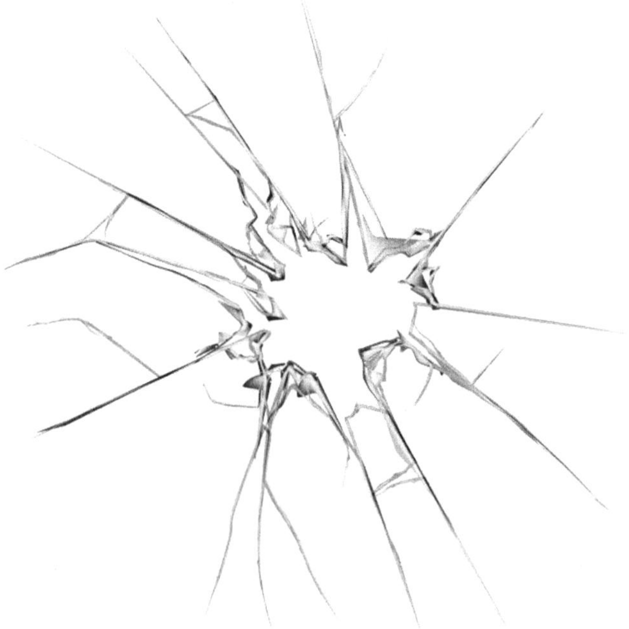

Self Love,

is a Practice, not a destination!!!

one love cracked me open

and ever since,

I treat tenderness like a threat.

It's not that I want to be alone.

It's that sometimes loneliness feels less dangerous than hoping

Someone might stay.

If my love was an ocean, yours was a bucket,
that too, an empty one.

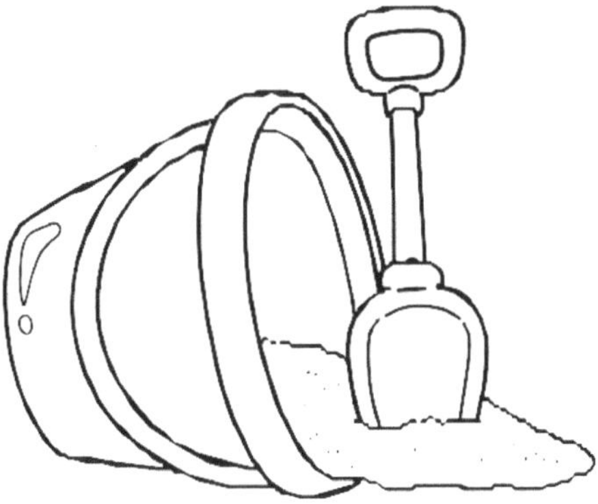

There was a time
I didn't want to peel my clothes off for him.
But he spoke in softness,
the kind that guilt-wraps your no until it sounds like yes.
He touched me
like a thief desperate for gold, but all he stole
was the glow I had left.
He peeled me open, not just skin, but soul...
like a demon looking for flesh behind the rarest eyes.
I lay there, bare and breaking,
searching for sunlight in a room growing darker with every breath he took.

My heart is so full of betrayals,
I can barely breathe in your loyalty.

How could you?

Words that never left my lips but slipped away from my mind.
I was lost in thoughts, wondering,
When was I not enough for you?
When did your love quietly fade, and why was I blind to see?
How did I miss the truth, in your counterfeit care,
forgetting the good that lived inside me?

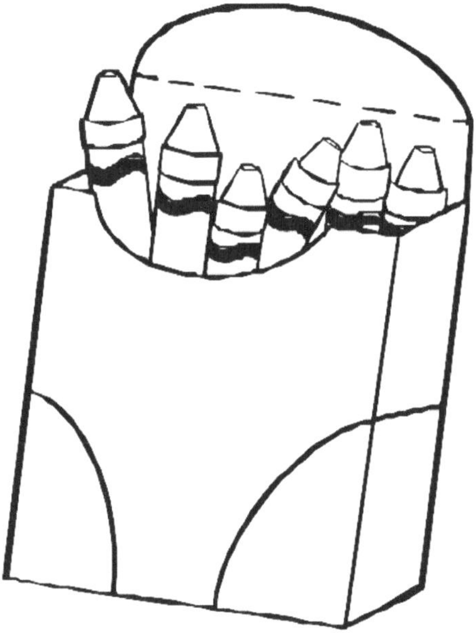

I loved you

with every crayon in the box, days spent coloring you in care.

But one drop of rain washed it all away.

There is a little girl in me, waiting for warm breezy summer to warm her heart, that was left cold.

I wanted to become a poetry, soft, flowing,

held in the warmth of someone's voice.

Instead,

you made me a poet, a sad one,

writing wounds into words, bleeding beauty from the ache.

I craved to be read like verses of love, not the author of heartbreak.

But here I am, inking sorrow into sunsets, turning silence into stanzas, because of the pain

was the only muse you left behind.